NORTHLEACH TO STOW ON THE WOLD

IN OLD PHOTOGRAPHS

THE YARD OF THE KINGS ARMS HOTEL in the centre of Stow-on-the-Wold early this century; truly 'a bit of old Stow'.

NORTHLEACH TO STOW ON THE WOLD

IN OLD PHOTOGRAPHS

COLLECTED BY

DAVID VINER

ALAN SUTTON

1987

Alan Sutton Publishing Limited
Brunswick Road · Gloucester

First published 1987

British Library Cataloguing in Publication Data

Northleach to Stow-on-the-Wold in old photographs.
1. Cotswold (Gloucestershire)——Social
life and customs——Pictorial works
I. Viner, D.J.
942.4'17081'0222 DA670.C83

ISBN 0–86299–399–7

front cover illustration:

The junction of the Northleach and Burford roads at the foot of Stow Hill in the years before the First World War. The Farmer's Arms continues to serve the needs of travellers along the Fosse Way which provides the link between the towns and villages collected in this volume. On the right are the entrance gates to Nether Swell Manor (Clift & Ryland of Stow).

Typesetting and origination by
Alan Sutton Publishing Limited.
Printed in Great Britain.
by WBC Print Limited · Bristol

CONTENTS

This volume is dedicated to the memory of my father, who knew these places.

Many of the photographs in this volume are the work of the Butt Studio at Bourton-on-the-Water, founded by W.J. Butt at the Bridge Studio (seen here) in the early 1920's and which flourishes under his successors to this day. The business moved to Lansdown in Bourton about 1928 and suffered a serious fire in 1934 when many of the original negatives were destroyed. However, large numbers of the photographs and postcards produced by the studio survive and it has been possible to rebuild something of the character of the business carried out all over the Cotswolds by William Butt (in the centre of this photograph), his wife Kathleen (on the left) and their manager Ernie Williams (on the right) who subsequently took over the business in 1947. Mr Butt's early experience in photography had been gained in the Royal Flying Corps.

Other photographers whose work is reproduced here include:

Clift & Ryland, Stow-on-the-Wold.
Frank Packer, Chipping Norton.
Percy Simms, Chipping Norton (including the Four Shire Series).
'Antona' Series.
Henry Taunt & Co., Oxford.
W. Dennis Moss, Cirencester (including the Cecily Series).
A.W. Teall, Northleach.
Barry Burge, Market Place, Northleach.
T. Powell, High Street, Bourton-on-the-Water.
A. Collett, Bourton-on-the-Water.
G. East, Post Office, Lower Slaughter.

INTRODUCTION

The three main centres featured in this volume all lie adjacent to the Fosse Way, the great Roman road bisecting Gloucestershire from north to south. Bourton-on-the-Water and Stow-on-the-Wold also have the distinction of occupying ancient British sites, created long before the Romans came, and Northleach has its own link with prehistory with its nearby Norbury Camp. With their long histories, all three places are filled with fascinating buildings of different ages, mostly built of the local Cotswold stone.

Their settings could not be more different. Stow bravely stands on top of a hill; Bourton lies among the lush water meadows of the River Windrush, while Northleach occupies a hollow in the wolds, entirely surrounded by breezy, rolling upland. At the dawn of the age of photography, a century or more ago, all three places were secluded and fairly self-contained. Today, they bask in the glare of the Cotswolds' booming tourist trade, particularly Bourton which is one of the most visited villages in the country.

It is this enormous increase in traffic that would most surprise an early photographer if he were to come back today. At Bank Holidays visitors have sometimes been turned away from Bourton because it is so full, and Stow's magnificent Square is often packed with cars. Only at Northleach has the pace eased with the welcome opening of a bypass in 1984. Old photographs can still remind us of how quiet it once was with leafy, bumpy lanes, solitary horse-drawn wagons and pedestrians having the road to themselves.

The first big improvement in transport came with the railway. Stow and Bourton stations were opened in 1862 and survived for a hundred years until the line was axed in 1962, but it was not until the 1930s that tourists began to arrive in large numbers, usually by charabanc. G.F. Moore was to a great extent responsible for the beautifying of Bourton in 1911. Then 'Bo' Morris opened his famous model village at the Old New Inn in 1937, and this set the seal on Bourton's fame as a tourist magnet. Harrington House, the most imposing house in the village, has been used as a hotel by the Holiday Fellowship since 1947.

The centre of Stow has also seen many changes since the first camera clicked. The gothic St Edward's Hall was built in 1878 and a horse pool at the junction of High Street and the Fosse Way was filled in and replaced by an ornamental drinking fountain in 1896, but the most dramatic change occurred in 1930 when the Cross House and adjoining building were demolished to open up the southern end of the Square. The latter was once the scene of vast sheep fairs but these have now been superseded by the twice-yearly horse fairs, famous throughout Britain. Other town halls were also rising: the Victoria Hall at Bourton in 1897 and the Cotswold Hall at Northleach in 1894, enhancing social life and the growth of local organisations. Bourton's first cottage hospital was only the third of its kind when built in 1861.

Of the three centres, Northleach has been unique in having its own grammar school, Westwood's, which occupied a site on the corner of the Farmington road from the end of the seventeenth century until 1902. After this the building became the offices of the Northleach Rural District Council until the latter's amalgamation with other local authorities to form Cotswold District Council in 1974. A new grammar school site was developed on the outskirts of the town between the wars and has been much expanded over the years.

Incidentally, Northleach and Stow are proud to be known as towns. Bourton, which is now bigger than either, is content to be called a village!

Each of these three main locations has its constellation of surrounding villages. Stow has the Swells, and other villages which unfortunately could not be included in this album. Bourton has the Rissingtons, consisting of Wyck Rissington, where Gustav Holst composer of 'The Planets' was organist from 1892–93; Little Rissington, where a large airfield was made in 1937, creating many jobs and Great Rissington, where a memorial in the church reminds us that Mrs W. Souls lost all five sons in the First World War. At Upper Slaughter all the men from the village returned safe and sound and none was lost in the Second World War either. Pretty Lower Slaughter must be the most photographed village in the Cotswolds.

Northleach is circled by Farmington, Hampnett, Eastington and just over the hills Aldsworth where the Garne family cherished their flock of Cotswold sheep over the centuries, the only survivors of the mighty breed that once made the Cotswolds rich. Happily a number of other flocks of Cotswolds have now been started from their stock.

The entire area remains predominantly agricultural though the tourist trade must now surpass farming as the biggest employer of labour. There has, of course, been quarrying for centuries and some of the stone houses built this century reveal that old standards of Cotswold craftsmanship have by no means been forgotten. The district continues as popular as ever with photographers!

Contributed by David Day

SECTION ONE

Northleach

NORTHLEACH PARISH CHURCH of St Peter & St Paul, one of the great wool churches of the Cotswolds, dating largely from the fifteenth century. Major benefactors included John Fortey who died in 1459 and his is one of the unique collection of wool merchants' brasses preserved in the church (Butt Studio).

BOX PEWS AND ORGAN beneath the tower before the restoration of 1877–84. The church has been restored again more recently with new seating designed by Sir Basil Spence and made by Gordon Russell (A.W. Teall of Northleach).

CHURCH PORCH, one of the crowning glories of Northleach and built in the first half of the fifteenth century (Butt Studio).

THE PRISON, NORTHLEACH, or more accurately a House of Correction, one of a number of new buildings erected in Gloucestershire in the 1780s as part of a programme of prison reform. The guiding light was Sir George Onesiphorus Paul, County High Sheriff in 1780 and magistrate, whose experience of the poor conditions in existing buildings so appalled him that he campaigned vigorously for improvements. These included a rebuilt county goal at Gloucester and four new houses of correction around the county.

At Northleach the chosen site was to the west of the town on the Fosse Way, where a high wall enclosed buildings laid out on a polygonal plan. The architect William Blackburn designed cell-blocks around a yard, with day cells on the ground floor and night cells above. The keeper's house was centrally placed to oversee all activities both within and without. Intended for 37 petty offenders, the house of correction remained in use from 1791 1857, after which with some rebuilding the site was used as a police station and magistrate's court until 1974. The surviving buildings, including a cell block, have been preserved as the Cotswold Countryside Collection, a museum of rural life and social history. In this view, from a postcard postmarked September 1910, the isolated nature of the site is clear at the junction of the Fosse Way and the Cheltenham to Oxford road (W. Dennis Moss of Cirencester).

'PRISON HILL' at the junction of the A40 and the Fosse Way, seen here climbing towards Bourton and with a remarkable absence of traffic. Local AA man, Mr Percy Adams of Northleach, controls the situation c. 1910 (Packer of Chipping Norton).

ACCIDENT AT THE CROSS ROADS right outside the police station c. 1923. For most of this century, this spot has been notorious for accidents which obviously occurred even when traffic was light. The new Northleach by-pass has at long last relieved the situation.

Two views of CLIFFORD & WEBB'S GARAGE AND FILLING STATION at the crossroads, opened on 21 May 1929 by Stan Webb and his friend Walter Clifford. They obtained the quarter-acre site for £60 and erected the wooden buildings which are seen here with pumps for BP, Texaco, Shell and Power petrols. In 1933 a new garage was constructed at a cost of £1,200 and erected around the original buildings which were then demolished. The lower view dates from June 1954 and shows the full period character of this building which still survives protected now by a modern canopy.

REBUILDING THE COTSWOLD HALL, 1894. The workmen of local builder William Mills of Fossebridge add an additional storey to the Northleach Institute and Reading Room in order to create the Cotswold Hall. The finance was raised by public subscription. The benefactor of the original building was local resident Mrs Elizabeth Stephenson, wife of a London bookmaker, whose love for Northleach was also expressed by funding an east window in the church and paying for pavements in the town. A library was attached to the reading room and still functions in public use but now as a snooker room. In her will of 1908 Mrs Stephenson left £1,000 to the trustees of the Institute for the benefit of the building. The Cotswold Hall continues in public use, and the building now has a fine period clock added in celebration of Queen Victoria's Diamond Jubilee in 1897 (Burge, Market Place, Northleach).

NORTHLEACH WEST END seen from the church tower *c.* 1910. The buildings of the town's brewery are clearly visible on the right. The main structure was reduced by one storey and the chimney demolished in 1950 when the derelict buildings were converted into a garage. On the left is Coalyard Farm and in the foreground on the far right the rear of the Cotswold Hall.

WEST END again, moving the camera around to the right and looking across the town to the north-east – a reminder of how close the fields came to the houses lining the main street of Northleach (Packer of Chipping Norton).

WEST END in 1897 with a display by Tayler's Northleach Brewery of barrels forming an arch across the street in celebration of Queen Victoria's Diamond Jubilee. The gates at the entrance to the brewery yard can be seen on the left, with, in the near foreground, the company's small 'off-licence'. The hanging sign advertises the Horse and Groom, a small pub which served this end of the town. Neatly framed in the archway is the Wheatsheaf Hotel, the next inn nearer the town centre. Note the state of the road which at this time was the main route between Oxford and Cheltenham (A.W. Teall of Northleach).

Another view of WEST END this time looking west away from the town centre (Taunt of Oxford, postmarked 1906).

NORTHLEACH D.D.S. & S. FÊTE parading along West End into the town on 7 August 1920. The barns and buildings of Coalyard Farm show very clearly on the right and also apparent is the open ditch which ran alongside the road here until the 1950s. The Discharged and Disabled Soldiers and Sailors Association resulted from the First World War and several views of similar fêtes are included in this volume (Butt of Bourton).

WHEATSHEAF HOTEL *c.* 1910. Immediately next door and with the small group of children outside was a sweet shop and seed merchants run by the Wilcox family. The timber-framed building is Kings Head Cottages, so named because the Kings Head Inn formerly stood next door. The building on the right is Walton House, used as veterinary stables for racehorses through most of the nineteenth century. The house gets its name from the horse Walton, son of a famous Derby winner (Packer of Chipping Norton).

BERT WILCOX and his father in the cart, the seed merchants and shop keepers in Northleach.

JOHN SLY, master wheelwright and undertaker of Northleach who contributed a great deal to the life of the town. Born at Sherborne in 1880, he wound up the church clock every day for ovcr 36 years until 1954, a task whlch involved a climb of 100 steps on each occasion. He was also a member of the Northleach tower of ringers for over 60 years. He died aged 95 in 1976 (Fox Photos).

NORTHLEACH COURT LEET has a long and distinguished history, its record book or Court Book surviving almost intact from 1543 to the present day. The medieval traditions of the hundred court managing the affairs of its area survived in the Court Leet at Northleach, where the ceremonial continues to the present day. A High Bailiff is elected annually. Here John Sly as one of the two Constables – and armed with the Constable's stave – posts the notice of the annual meeting on the door of the Old Lock Up next to the town's post office in the Market Place (Fox Photos).

STOCKS AND PILLORY in the Market Place, erected as a contribution to the Festival of Britain celebrations of 1951, the highlight of which was a medieval pageant. This reconstruction was the work of Alfred Wellman, handicrafts master at Westwoods Grammar School. Removed the following year, the stocks are still sought out by visitors seeking a piece of medieval Northleach history! (Butt Studio).

A SERIES OF STUDIES OF THE TOWN c. 1904 BY HENRY TAUNT OF OXFORD (possibly taken together) and sold very successfully for many years as postcards. Captioned 'Bird's Eye View', this scene shows the splendid situation of the church seen from south of the town, the chimney of the brewery visible beyond (Taunt & Co. 233).

HIGH STREET or the north side of the Market Place showing clearly the various styles of Cotswold architecture. The double-gables of Gardiner's Cotswold Printers is probably seventeenth century; nearer to the camera is an eighteenth-century façade. Looking east (Taunt & Co. 344).

WEST END with the entrance to the brewery on the left. The golden balls and the ornate iron gates were a feature of this part of the town until they were sold in 1950 for £100. The Cotswold Hall is obscured by the trees on the right (Taunt & Co. 1339).

EAST END looking back towards the town centre and again with an almost total absence of traffic. The inn sign advertises the Prince of Wales Inn, closed in the 1950s (Taunt & Co. 1338).

NORTHLEACH CYCLISTS outside the Union Hotel in High Street at the turn of the century. In the centre of the group is Mr Albert Earle, long-time Northleach citizen and church organist with the only bowler hat in the party. Note the wall plaque of the Cyclists Touring Club. Present day Northleach Olde Tyme Wheelers maintain this leisure tradition (Burge, Market Place, Northleach).

AN EARLY VIEW OF THE 1890s of a fête or flower show in the Vicarage Field. A number of floats can be discerned and the band is on hand to provide entertainment (F. Mortimer Savory, Cirencester).

WANE, DRAPER AND GROCER in the Market Place *c.* 1890. One of the ladies in the group is Miss Clara Maretha Soul, the shop milliner.

ERECTING THE NEW LINE OF DOUBLE-POST TELEGRAPH POLES through Northleach in 1907. The line stood alongside the A40 Oxford to Cheltenham Road for many years and formed a well-known landmark. An interesting group is attracted by the event outside the Union Hotel.

PROCLAMATION OF KING GEORGE V IN 1911. The crowd assembled in the Market Place includes Canon Jones, prominent local citizen John Bowl, and Mr Godwin the headmaster of Westwoods Grammar School and a one-time High Bailiff of Northleach. One of the two constables with the staves is Mr William Lea of Winterwell Farm, a local farmer, steam roller proprietor and threshing contractor. Note the shutters to Eltome & Co, the grocer's shop behind the group (Barry Burge, Northleach).

JOHN BOWL, proprietor of Eltome & Bowl, local businessman in Northleach and sometime High Bailiff of the town. Here he is outside his home at Greystones in West End with his housekeeper Miss Day.

FLOWER SHOW held on 14 August 1913 in the Vicarage Grounds in beautiful weather and it was reported in the local press that 'the show was a very good one'. Entertainments included the Boy Scouts in an Indian play, represented here by Mr Arthur Moss of Leygore Manor, Turkdean (standing) and Wolfred Blackwell on the ground (Percy Simms, Chipping Norton).

BOY SCOUTS OF NORTHLEACH AND DISTRICT line up for a photo call, armed with a small cannon. At the time this photograph was taken, the Scout movement in Britain was only a few years old.

NORTHLEACH SCHOOL, standards Two and Three in June 1915. Amongst the faces are: (back row) Philip Dore, –?–, Vera Clayton, –?–, –?–, Arthur Cook; (third row back) –?–, Mavis Blackwell, Sonny Hooper, Daisy Hale, –?–, Ada Cook, Harold Stevens, Sydney Hughes; (second row) Ida Hughes, –?–, Ethel Newcombe, Gwendoline Leach, Ivy Hale, Lucy Hall, Edie Cook, Dolly Haines, Fred Mustoe; (front row) Dennis Hill, Edward Butler, Charlie Clark, Bill Ricketts, Sydney Cook, Robert Hyde, –?–, –?–, and Frank Cook (Butt Studio).

NORTHLEACH CHOIR *c.* 1906. Standing, rear: Frank Cole, Lionel Burge, Charles Howse, Jack Cook, Harold Painter, Thomas Buffin and Sidney Groves. Seated, middle row: Reginald Stephens, Edward Haines, Robert Cook, Charles Westmacott and Wilfrid Blackwell. Front row: Charles Cook, Victor Hayward, — Aston, — Aston and Alfred Cook.

MARKET PLACE, looking west, with the Union Hotel prominent in the street scene. Note the prominent double telegraph poles marching through the town (from a ?Butt Studio postcard purchased in 1924).

TWO VIEWS OF THE MARKET PLACE on the same day in the mid 1920s with the triangular nature of the open area clearly visible; the war memorial was erected in 1922. Jack Hills' cycle and motor agents business is well advertised next to the Union Hotel (Packer of Chipping Norton).

FÊTE DAY AGAIN in Northleach on behalf of the Discharged and Disabled Soldiers and Sailors Association. Here a good crowd supports the parade as it passes the Wheatsheaf Hotel, 'tourists' headquarters' (Butt of Bourton).

THE GATHERING OF THE PARADE for the fête in the Market Place on 7 August 1920 (Butt of Bourton).

UNVEILING THE WAR MEMORIAL on 3 June 1922 with an appropriate parade and a small crowd of onlookers. Across the Market Place is the Sherborne Arms (Butt of Bourton).

NORTHLEACH FLOWER SHOW in the Vicarage Field on 19 August 1920, just under a fortnight after the quite separate D.D.S. & S. fête in the preceding photographs. There are memories of an earlier and similar event on page 25 (Butt of Bourton).

ENTERTAINMENT by The Double D's at the Flower Show. The card was printed quickly, as this copy was posted from Northleach on 1 September by one of the members of the audience (Butt of Bourton).

MORRIS DANCERS performing on the cricket field, the other popular place for public gatherings in Northleach. The date is 1923 and the group consists of: back row, Ronald Hayward, Lionel Burge, Frank Cook, Jack Cook with the emblem, Sidney Cook, Percy Haines and his brother Reginald Haines; (front row seated) Alice Rayer, 'Pem' Leach, Kitty Banks, Miss Godwin, Madam Hill, Molly Cole, Doris Rayer and Maud Stroud. On the ground are Mary Viveash, Hilda Rolstan, Mavis Blackwell and Miss Stephens. Seated on the right is Albert Earle, musician and church organist (Bull of Bourton).

THE DANCERS perform for the assembled audience on the same day, 6 August 1923 (Butt of Bourton).

NORTHLEACH SCOUT BAND ready to provide entertainment at a Flower Show. Again prominent in the line-up is Bert Earle, seen here in his role of bandmaster (Percy Simms, Chipping Norton).

WI OUTING TO OXFORD, possibly the first outing after the formation of Northleach WI, in the mid 1920s. Here the gathering poses in front of one of the college gates, with Madam Hill of College House, Northleach in the centre foreground. She was a founder member and a keen organiser of local activities, including folk dancing (Soame of Oxford).

HIGH STREET looking east in the 1920s and with a number of interesting features. On the immediate left, the Red Lion Inn is seen before the days of exposed timberwork to its upper storey. Next door is the Congregational Chapel and to the right Millers, a saddlers business. In the centre distance is the Great House, one of the finest buildings in the town and largely demolished in the winter of 1936/7 (Percy Simms of Chipping Norton 'Four Shire Series').

BOBBY HYDE, the telegraph boy in Northleach, seen here outside the Post Office, in 1922 at the age of 16.

OUTING FROM NORTHLEACH to the Wembley Empire Exhibition of 1924. In the coach are (left to right standing): Selina Tuckwell, Edith Leach, Mr & Mrs Tom Leach, George, Harry and Mrs Haines, Mrs Hughes, Mrs Ted Leach, Elsie Leach, Mr & Mrs Harry Leach, Alan Clayton (at the rear), Hilda Rolston, Mrs E. Mustoe and Mrs Siford. Seated: Eva and Maggie Cook, Carol Hyde with Mr & Mrs William Cook, Beatie Tea with Mrs Westmacott, George Tuckwell and Albert Leach, –?– with John Siford. In front: –?–, Leonard Tyson, Gwen Leach, Kitty Banks, Mrs Fred Cook, Reg Haines and Mr Fred Cook. The driver is Mr Coates. On this occasion at Wembley four of the Leach family met their parents who worked in a hospital at Watford.

'THE PEEP' linking the Green with East End, and seen here looking towards the church and Church Farm. The first building on the left housed Albert Price's blacksmith's shop. At the time of this photograph, the roadway had not been made up and the drainage channels are apparent ('Antona' series, Chipping Norton).

THE PEEP AGAIN, but at an earlier date and probably c. 1904. A hanging sign advertises the Kings Head and the limewash on the cottage on the right reveals its seventeenth century architectural details (Taunt & Co 346).

CHARLES BLACKWELL outside Church Farm before the alterations to the building in 1911. He was a haulier and also held the mail contract for the Post Office, delivering parcels and letters between Cheltenham and Northleach in his horse-drawn van (A.W. Teall of Northleach).

THE GREEN, the other part of what was once a large open market place in Northleach when the town was laid out early in the thirteenth century. The process of rebuilding the cottages at centre left was interrupted by wartime use as a small factory (Butt of Bourton).

TUDOR HOUSE at The Green, one of the most interesting historical buildings in the town. It is believed to be the home of John Fortey, whose wealth paid for much of the enlargement of Northleach church in the fifteenth century, although the building probably dates from a century earlier. A butcher's shop has occupied the left-hand side all this century, being Nichols before Castles (Packer of Chipping Norton).

NORTHLEACH SCOUTS, performing at a fête on 8 May 1930. Standing at the rear are performers Ewart Cook, –?–, Ronald Wearing, Horace Cook, Llew Sly, Maurice Miller, Mary Smith, Ronald Mustoe, Anthony Leech (at rear), Harold Siford, Jack Bennett with, in front, Albert and Frank Barrett. In the middle row are Revd de Lacy Mann, curate and scoutmaster, Cyril Sly, assistant scoutmaster, Edward Leach, Victor Hunt, Charlie Leach, Jack Clayton, Mrs Agg and Jim Berry. The front row consists of George Tea, William Leach, John Webley, Victor and Frank Mustoe, Ivor Miller, Cyril Leech, Eric Blackwell, Frank Dodge and Leslie Bennett (Butt of Bourton).

MARKET PLACE in the 1930s with the pump house prominent in the foreground. This was removed during the war. Also notable is the fine period telephone box and the presence of one of the ubiquitous Black & White Coaches which were a regular feature of Northleach traffic *en route* along the A40 from Cardiff to London. Beyond are two baker's shops, Spencers and Youngs, which, together with Nichols the butchers on The Green, gave rise to the Northleach saying for good food: 'Nichol's Sausages, Young's Banbury Cakes and Spencer's Lardy Cakes' (Percy Simms of Chipping Norton).

VIEW ACROSS THE MARKET PLACE towards the church, giving a sense of the close relationship between the church and the buildings of the town centre. The post office occupies the central position here, with the tiny lock-up to its left (Butt of Bourton).

GATHERING IN THE MARKET PLACE in 1931 for a meet of the Heythrop Hunt, outside Billie's Cafe and the Sherborne Arms. From left to right: Mrs Brooks, matron at the Northleach Hospital, –?–, Mr Brooks, master at the Hospital, — Adams, Bill Cole, Llew Sly, Maurice Miller, Ada Cook, and in the foreground John Wane and Charlie Cowley. On the right are Harry Young, Butcher Wheeler and George Mustoe. Both car and horse belonged to the Revd Hodson (Frank Packer of Chipping Norton).

WESTWOOD'S GRAMMAR SCHOOL, founded in the town following a bequest of Hugh Westwood in 1559 and a survivor until the present day's reorganisation of education resources. After various homes in the town, these buildings were established at the east end of Northleach in 1927 (Butt of Bourton).

NORTHLEACH C. OF E. SCHOOL in 1935. Back row: William Lyford, Desmond Mustoe, Bernard Iles, Donald Busby and Cyril Morss, Middle row: Raymond Leach, Norman Hunt, Kenneth Legg, Sidney Mustoe, Kenneth Clayton, Percy Fields and Kenneth Pink. Front row: Ivy Day, Rosalind Haines, Enid Sly, Audrey Dore, Doreen Norman, Miss Edna Ball form-mistress, Winifred Freeman, Joyce Hanks, Patricia Tingley, Norah Leach and Ruth Clayton. At the rear is headmaster Sidney T.J. Turner (Scholastic Souvenir Co. Ltd. Blackpool).

NORTHLEACH FOOTBALL CLUB, winners of the Bourton Hospital Cup in 1936–37. Standing at the back are Revd Hodson, Ernest Tuckwell, Charlie Stevens, Reg Green, Bill Leach, Albert Larner, Bunny Goodall, Jack Tuckwell and Bill Norman. In the centre are Jetlow Larner, Bill Pearce and Les Tuckwell, and at the front, Albert Barrett, Horace Cook, Bert Leach, Teddy Margetts and Ron Wearing sen. (Butt of Bourton).

NORTHLEACH CRICKET CLUB in 1936. Standing at the back are umpire S. Cook, W.G. Leach, H.A. Cook, E.C. Wearne, J. le P. Webb, A.W. Miles, second umpire W.F. Brooks and scorer R. Miles. In the front row: W.P. Bassett, E.W. Hutt, captain A.V. Smart, A.E. Leach, S.T.J. Turner and hon. sec. A.F. Barrett (Butt of Bourton).

MARKET PLACE AND EAST END of the town as seen from the church tower. The form of the medieval open space can be appreciated with buildings subsequently infilling to create the present pair of open areas. East End is here largely two rows of houses against the street with open fields behind. Only the workhouse forms a distinguishable group at the edge of the town ('Antona' series).

CORONATION DAY in May 1937 with a procession forming up outside the Wheatsheaf Hotel. Court Leet constables John Sly and Mr Eustace parade the staves with Dr. Bowen-Jones between them and his son John as mascot. The Mother's Union banner is also on parade, followed by the Girl Guides and the British Legion.

ROYAL OBSERVER CORPS at the Northleach post in 1942. Part of 24 Group ROC, with a call sign 'love-four', the wooden building was situated half a mile west of the town and had a full-time contingent. On parade here are (back row) Obs. H. Leach, Obs. S. Smith, Obs. A. Last, L/Obs. W.G. Leishman and Obs. W. Morss; (front row) Obs. J. Norman, Obs. H. Roungvell, Obs. Offr. B. Barwell, Chf. Offr. H. Hallinan and Obs. H.C. Cook.

SPECIAL CONSTABULARY, Northleach Section during the years of the Second World War. In the back row are Special Constables J. Sly, L.W. Burge, P. Greaves, G. Westmacott and E.G. Holland; in the middle row O. Leach, E.J. Richens, E.G. Jones, W.G. Leach, L.F. Wearing and J. Leach. Seated are Specials C.H. Gloster and W.V. Blackwell flanking PCs S.T. Smith and H. Elliott, with Special Sergeant S.T.J. Turner in the centre (Butt of Bourton).

ST JOHNS AMBULANCE BRIGADE, Northleach branch outside Westwood's Grammar School during the Second World War, having won the cup in the county first aid competition.

NORTHLEACH UNION, or workhouse, built to one of the standard designs of the day by George Wilkinson of Witney and opened *c.* 1836. The word Union refers to the amalgamation of parishes served by the Poor Law Union, from which model the local government pattern developed later in the century. As usual, an imposing façade hides more utilitarian architecture behind (W.J. Butt, Bridge Studio, Bourton-on-the-Water).

RE-DEDICATION SERVICE at the chapel of the Northleach Public Institution (formerly workhouse) on Saturday 16 November 1946. From left to right are Mr Woodward, Mr Norfolk (county public assistance officer) Mr Heale, Mrs Price, and Mr W.P. Bassett. The choir consisted of Enid Sly, Alice Hall, Ethel Jones, 'Pem' Leach, Mrs F. Hann, Joyce Sly and Jack Acock. At the rear is Revd Stentiford of the Congregational Chapel.

COURT LEET MEMBERS observing the traditions of centuries in the Wheatsheaf Hotel at the annual meeting *c.* 1950. From left to right: Clifford Pearce, Northleach RDC rating officer; Herbert Williams, RDC fuel officer; Bill Cook, builder; Charlie Young, baker. At the rear Alfred Ward, clerk to RDC who retired in 1951; in front Harry Barrett, butcher; Bill Miles, registrar; Lord Bathurst of Cirencester Park, Lord of the Leet; Howard St G. Rawlins, solicitor of Cirencester and High Steward; Ernest Brookes, master of the Poor Law Institution/Hospital; George Mason, farmer of Church Farm: John Sly, wheelwright and undertaker; Reg Siford of the Red Lion Inn; Dr. Edward Bowen-Jones, physician and surgeon; Maurice Miller, draper; Stan Webb, garage proprietor and Alfred Wellman, handicrafts master at Westwood's.

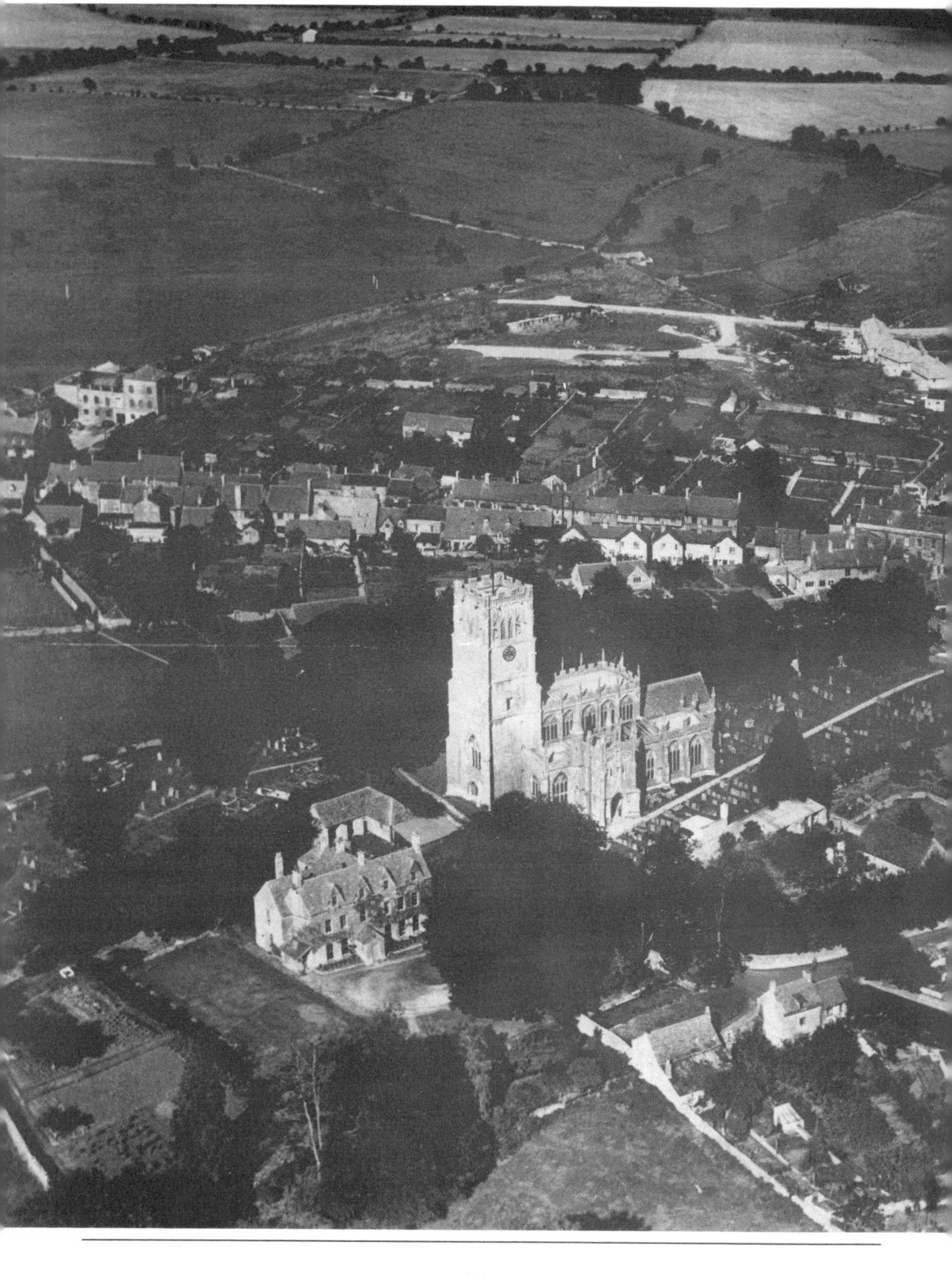

NORTHLEACH FROM THE AIR, photographed between 1952 and 1957. Even at this date, the relatively concentrated nature of the town is clear in this view which looks north. Centrepiece remains the parish church and alongside it the vicarage and cemetery behind. To the right not all of the Market Place can be seen, but there is a good view of West End throughout most of its length from the Brewery to the town centre. Beyond, the major post-war building scheme in Northleach is taking shape: the Walton council housing estate. The staged nature of this development can be seen and helps to date the photograph; the road pattern is largely in place but not all the houses have been begun. The same scene today would show the line of the new by-pass across the entire rear of the picture from left to right and a growing degree of housing infilling which marks the increasing pace of life in Northleach in the later 1980s.

CONGREGATIONAL CHAPEL in the corner of the Market Place, seen here in 1903. Opened in 1860, this small congregation celebrated its centenary only shortly before closing down in the 1960s. On the left is the Red Lion Inn, a fine timber-framed building and on the right Giles & Son's stores (Taunt of Oxford).

BUS SHELTER AND PUBLIC CONVENIENCE combined in the Market Place and the centre of great public controversy when it was first projected in the late 1950s. After a public enquiry at which the proposal was described as 'sheer vandalism', the building was constructed for Northleach RDC in traditional materials and completed in 1961. The stone came from the nearby Farmington stone quarry. The 171 bus on the right is a remainder of a long-standing bus route into Cheltenham.

SECTION TWO

Villages west of the Fosse: Hampnett Notgrove Turkdean Hazleton & Salperton Cold Aston

PERSEVERANCE outside the Puesdown Inn on the A40 coaching route from Northleach to Cheltenham, in the days before the arrival of the motor bus. George Hayward of Hampnett operated the run plus a four-in-hand coach to Oxford as well. He sold out to Black & White Coaches and died in 1939.

HAMPNETT TURN on the Fosse Way just above the Northleach cross-roads in the winter of 1916.

HAMPNETT COTTAGES before the First World War. The scene is a classic view of the harmony of Cotswold stone with the landscape (Percy Simms of Chipping Norton 'Four Shire Series').

HAMPNETT CHURCH OF ST GEORGE which retains much of its original Norman character. It has an especial attraction in the wall decoration by its Victorian rector Revd Wiggin c. 1871 which captures something of how a medieval church interior might have looked (Taunt & Co. 1151).

RETURNING HOME. Three teams of working horses return to the farm at the end of the working day in 1935. Hampnett church tower is prominent on the right and note too the thatch roof of the farm buildings – thatch was more commonly used in the Cotswolds than is appreciated today (M. Wight – Museum of English Rural Life).

SHEEP SHEARING on Mr J.A. McArthur's Manor Farm at Hampnett on 4 June 1956. The shepherds are R. Phillips and J. Wilson (Museum of English Rural Life).

NOTGROVE, a charming village study in the 1920s, almost certainly achieved by W.J. Butt on his bicycle from Bourton-on-the-Water (Butt Studio).

NOTGROVE MANOR, an impressive view through the wrought iron gates. This seventeenth century house suffered from a fire and has been largely rebuilt. Notgrove is a typical Cotswold estate village.

OUTSIDE THE WHEELWRIGHT'S SHOP on Notgrove village green in 1937. Fine traditional Cotswold farm wagons await attention. Also traditional is the spelling of the county name on the headboard (Museum of English Rural Life).

LOADING MILK CHURNS at Mr P. Webster Cory's Manor Farm at Notgrove between the wars (Museum of English Rural Life).

NOTGROVE STATION on the Kingham Junction to Cheltenham line, a section completed in 1881 on the through route of the Banbury & Cheltenham Railway. Notgrove was reputed to be the highest through station on the Great Western Railway at over 760 ft. above sea level. Another GWR tradition was the distance from the village – well over a mile!

LEYGORE FARM at Turkdean. These two views were taken *c.* 1885 before the building was redeveloped as a manor house. The family group is particularly interesting because it is a reminder of some of the most long-established Cotswold farming families: the Hewers, Garnes, Minchins, Walkers, and Taylers of Eastington, Aldsworth, Hazelton, Sherborne, Farmington and Northleach. Here are George Hewer and his wife Elizabeth (née Garne) with some of their family of seven sons and six daughters.

EDWARD WHEELER, who delivered mail by bicycle and later by pony and trap to Hazleton, Salperton and Compton Abdale. The post was brought from Cheltenham by the Northleach carrier and left in the postman's hut at Hazleton Pike.

JOHNNY HOPKINS, the village church fiddler at Salperton who played for services until his death in 1948.

HAZLETON village and church in the early years of this century (Taunt & Co. 1514).

SALPERTON, the village school and cottages. Are the children holding the photographer's bicycle?

SALPERTON WAR MEMORIAL, 1919. Unusual in the Cotswolds as a wooden Calvary instead of a stone cross, and interesting too in its roadside situation away from the village buildings (Butt of Bourton).

CHURCH AND VILLAGE SCENE at Cold Aston, a village which gives an impression of remoteness more apparent than real. The village name adds to this feeling; originally Aston, it became Cold Aston in 1255 and Aston Blank in 1535. Now it is officially Cold Aston once again (Powell of Bourton-on-the-Water, postmarked 1917).

VILLAGE SCENE at Cold Aston, looking towards the pub and the church (Royal Standard Photo Co., Evesham C119).

VILLAGE CENTRE at Cold Aston with the Plough Inn on the left; a companion view to the previous photograph.

ROLLING with a pair of horses in Cold Aston parish in fields close to the Fosse Way at Gilbert's Grave (Eric Guy colln., Museum of English Rural Life).

SECTION THREE

Bourton-on-the-Water

THE CLASSIC VILLAGE VIEW OF BOURTON-ON-THE-WATER, which owes its appeal to visitors to a combination of the river Windrush and picturesque village buildings. These photographs show Bourton before the commercialism which has changed its character today. Here High Bridge dates from 1756. Its older name is Town Hall Bridge, a reference to the Victoria Hall on the left, built in 1897 (A. Collett of Bourton).

MILL BRIDGE with the wagon from Wilkin's the millers leaving the corn mill which is off the picture to the left. The building beyond the horses dates from 1902 and was built as a shop (A. Collett of Bourton).

HIGH STREET with a row of shops including Lodges, drapers; Wilkins, bakers and Phillips the blacksmith. Bourton benefactor George Moore demolished part of the building on the right to create access for the building of Moore Road in the 1930s.

BERNARD PHILLIPS, blacksmith in the High Street, leading a horse through the front door of the house from the smithy behind.

A LATER VIEW showing the front door from the previous photograph on the left and next to it Moore Road. The village war memorial occupies a dominant position on the green (Butt of Bourton).

ON THE BANKS OF THE RIVER looking towards High Bridge and the war memorial. On the right, the copse of trees which had dominated this part of the village centre was removed in 1936 (Butt of Bourton).

TWO MORE VIEWS of the best known part of Bourton-on-the-Water. Payne's footbridge dates from 1776, whilst the larger road bridge dates from 1911 and is another example of the benefaction of George Moore, whose initials 'G.W.M.' adorn the keystone along with the date. His home was Chardwar, just around the corner from these views (Butt of Bourton and T. Powell of Bourton).

A COMPANION VIEW SHOWING BOTH HIGH BRIDGE AND NEW BRIDGE BEYOND, and dating between 1911 and the building of the war memorial in 1921. On the left are Fosters, grocers and drapers; Gilberts, grocers; and Hartwells, ironmongers. Hartley House beyond provides Bourton with one of its more stylish buildings (Powell of Bourton, postmarked 1912).

MOORE COTTAGE HOSPITAL, opened in Moore Road in 1928 and a further debt owed to George Moore. This view was taken soon after opening and shows the classic details of a small cottage hospital, which survives largely unaltered today. Note the patients in the fresh air but protected by the porticos on either wing (Butt of Bourton).

THE MODEL VILLAGE was opened on 12 May 1937, a one-ninth scale model of Bourton in the grounds of the Old New Inn. The inspiration of landlord 'Bo' Morris, the village was created by local craftsmen and in local materials, transforming a hobby into an ambitious project. Eventually funding proved a problem, soon resolved by opening the model to visitors at a charge of sixpence. Now the attraction is one of the main features of Bourton life. This Butt Studio series of postcard views must have sold thousands since they were first printed! (Butt of Bourton).

MODEL VILLAGE: two more views from the Butt series, including a representation of St Lawrence's Church (Butt of Bourton).

MR HUMPHRIES, a haulier in Bourton with his family at Lyncroft Field *c.* 1920.

LANSDOWN at Bourton. A view from the church tower, looking towards the Fosse Way. Bartlett's boot and shoe warehouse is well advertised on a group of houses not constructed until after 1895 when this side of the road was open ground (postmarked 1906).

UPPER MILL or Lansdown Mill, formerly a fulling mill and surviving in use as a mill until *c.* 1927 (postmarked 1920).

ST LAWRENCE'S CHURCH, a Georgian church replacing the earlier Norman building. The tower of *c.* 1784 is a fine example of its type with a lead-covered dome, balustrades and decorative urns at each corner. The lozenge clock face dates from 1785 and the clock proper was dedicated on 3 February 1911 – it cost £360 (Butt Studio, postmarked 1914).

FLOWER SHOW at Bourton in August 1919 with Mr Humphries in bowler hat and beard amongst the group seated on the hurdles (Butt of Bourton).

COLLETT'S general stores in Lansdown which continued trading in this position until about 25 years ago. The building is in two parts; to the original 1894 right hand side was added a new section in 1911 and here the respective shop fronts reflect these dates. A splendid representation of the larger type of village shop (A. Collett of Bourton).

TOM WHITING, the Bourton wheelwright and his assistant Fred Whiting completing work on a wheel at their shop in Lansdown in 1941. The implement being used to hold the wheel tight while the iron strakes are secured is called a 'samson'. Inside the workshop William Oakey and Fred Whiting work on another wheel.

CLUB DAY in Bourton, held on the first Friday in June, was an annual festivity for various societies and represents a fine Costwold village tradition now largely forgotten. Village friendly societies celebrated with a procession, a lunch or dinner and some sports or entertainment. Here on 7 June 1907 the Chedworth Brass Band prepares to lead the procession of the Conservative Benefit Society from the church gates to the New Inn (A. Collett of Bourton).

CLUB DAY AGAIN, but a few years later on 4 June 1920 and outside the New Inn. Many such festivities died out after the Great War; at Bourton traditional Club Days continued until c. 1930. Note the staves on parade and the largely male gathering (Butt of Bourton).

STATION YARD at Bourton-on-the-Water at the turn of the century, with plenty of activity in evidence. This view captures the essentially rural nature of the railway scene, with tiny offices for the various businesses, a horse-drawn wagon on the weigh-bridge and various workmen on parade. The station building and the goods shed belong to the early days of the railway which was opened to Bourton from Kingham Junction in 1862. Note too the conveyances for passengers between station and village.

BOURTON STATION. A late view, from c. 1934, and just prior to the demolition of the original timber-framed building and its replacement (as also at Stow-on-the-Wold station) with a new building in Cotswold stone, which incidentally has survived the closure of the line some 25 years ago.

ANNUAL FEAST of the Heythrop Hunt Keepers and Earthstoppers, held at the Railway Hotel at Bourton on 26 April 1907. Alex Stokey, landlord, was a keen supporter of the Hunt. The Hotel stables and yard can be seen to the right of the group, which manages to include the village postman! (A. Collett of Bourton).

STATION ROAD, with the Baptist church prominent on the left, and an air of rural calm.

FLOODING in Clapton Row at Bourton, caused by heavy rain on 31 May 1924. Hartwells showroom can be detected beyond the bushes to the right (Butt of Bourton).

NEW INN in a charming and rustic composition looking towards the village in the early years of this century. The New Inn was built as such in 1718 and has a sundial of this date inscribed to Silas Wells. It became the Old New Inn in 1930. The nearer building served Bourton as its Assembly Rooms for a number of years.

A SIMILAR VIEW from across the river Windrush with the Assembly Rooms just visible behind the tree (Powell of Bourton, postmarked 1915).

MILLER'S WAGON in the yard of Lower Mill at Bourton, which continued as a corn mill until recent years. Here the miller's lad Tom Margetts parades a pair of horses harnessed to a fine example of a miller's wagon, which included amongst its duties a period of Army service during the Great War.

T. & H. WILKINS, the family business of millers, bakers and grocers established in Bourton in the nineteenth century and still in good health when this record photograph was taken in the mill yard between the wars. Several of the Wilkins family are in the group; so too is Tom Margetts from the previous photograph, seen here second from left in the front with arms folded (Butt of Bourton).

THE AVENUE, a fine stand of elm trees and looking, in this scene, away from the church towards the railway station. Now the trees have all gone and Bourton Vale School and Bourton Primary School occupy the grounds to the left (T. Powell of Bourton, postmarked 1914).

DISMANTLING THE GUN EMPLACEMENT in the centre of Bourton on 20 February 1937. Following the Great War, a German army field gun was given to the village by Col. Sinnott, but was not displayed until after at least seven years of active correspondence with the parish council. Erected in 1927, the gun was removed for scrap about 1935 and this scene records the final chapter in an interesting episode of Bourton history (Butt of Bourton).

CONCERT by the children of Bourton in aid of the Red Cross on 28 May 1941, which raised a sum of £12. The group is seen here outside the Rectory (Butt of Bourton).

SECTION FOUR

In and Around the Windrush Valley:

Farmington
Sherborne
Windrush
Great & Little Barrington
Great & Little Rissington
Wyck Rissington
Clapton-on-the-Hill

EDMUND WHEELER who worked for the Northleach Rural District Council as a roadman under Mr Viveash.

FARMINGTON SCHOOL in 1928, in the back row: Bill Coates, Cecil Bartlett, Billy Green, Gwendoline Musty, Gwen Green, Mary Jerome, Billy Musty and Kenny Green. In the front: Benjamin Musty, Norah Newman, Cyril Morss, Sam Morss, Edmund Groves, Denis Hayward, George Jerome, Frank Musty, Frank Robins, Bill Lyford and Renee Lyford.

FARMINGTON, the green and the well house of 1874, a village focal point (Taunt & Co 1466).

BUS SHELTER, an award-winning design in a Festival of Britain competition in 1951 for enterprising village activities to celebrate the occasion. Taking its octagonal theme from the pump or well-house in the village, the bus shelter was built of local stone given from the village quarries and erected by local labour. A plaque records this achievement.

FUNERAL OF JAMES BLACKWELL, farmer and threshing contractor who died at Upper End, Eastington on 19 January 1947 at the age of 83. His obituary described him as 'a well-known figure in the Cotswold agricultural world. He had a wide knowledge of agricultural machinery and as proprietor of a great deal of threshing tackle he undertook threshing operations for a large number of farmers in the district.' These scenes are remarkable as recording a long-standing country tradition, the conveyance of the coffin on the family's best farm wagon to the church. In the capable hands of the Sly family of undertakers, the cortège leaves Eastington with Cyril and Llew Sly assisted by Messrs Hardiman and Westmacott. In the lower picture the entrance to James Blackwell's former home at Empshill Farm at Farmington is passed on the long and slow journey to Farmington church. Local memories recall the bitterly cold day (Allaways, Photographers, 164, High Street, Cheltenham).

SHERBORNE HOUSE, one of the great houses of the Windrush valley and home of the Dutton family whose influence in Gloucestershire society was considerable. The earlier mansion was largely rebuilt in the first half of the nineteenth century, but by the Second World War had ceased to be a country home on the grand scale. It has recently been converted into luxury flats. Alongside, the church of St Mary Magdalene is cheek by jowl with the great house and rctains the close associations with the family (Hooper of Swindon, postmarked 1910).

'CHELTENHAM LODGES', the formal entrance to Sherborne Park from the Oxford to Cheltenham road and part of the nineteenth-century adornments (Packer of Chipping Norton).

LODGE PARK, designed not as a house but as a grandstand from which to view the coursing of deer by greyhounds on the Sherborne estate. John Dutton acquired land to form a deer park in 1624–40 and Lodge Park dates from sometime after this period. In 1898 it was converted into a house by the then Lady Sherborne and was the family home in preference to Sherborne House after 1940.

GARDENERS at Sherborne House, under the charge of head gardener Mr Mitchell, line up with some of the tools of their trade (Percy Simms of Chipping Norton).

'EDGCOTE CLIPPER', a two year old bull on Mr Stratton's farm at Sherborne in March 1918.

SHERBORNE SCHOOL group *c.* 1890 and one of the earliest such groups to be included in this volume (R. Slade, High Street, Cheltenham).

SHERBORNE CLUB DAY on Whit Tuesday 1913. The Union Jack is prominent at the head of the parade with Chedworth Silver Band behind, as the procession begins to draw up in front of the lodge at the village entrance to Sherborne House. Behind is the impressive stable building with the river Windrush beyond. The procession is *en route* from the church to the school field, where sports and entertainment were provided. The friendly societies here were the Free Foresters and the Oddfellows (Percy Simms of Chipping Norton).

1913 CLUB DAY. The organising committee is not short of numbers and includes (centre front) Mr Grey, agent to the Sherborne Estate and (far left) Mr Tom Matthews, secretary to the Club. In the lower view are wives and children forming a group at the Club Day festivities (Percy Simms of Chipping Norton).

A LATER CLUB DAY IN SHERBORNE, this time on 28 May 1920. Such gatherings were important features of the village calendar, a mixture of companionship and simple pleasures (Butt of Bourton).

FLOWER SHOW in 1913, with a cricket match as a special attraction between Mr Grey's XI from Sherborne and Mr Garne's XI from Aldsworth (Percy Simms of Chipping Norton).

SHERBORNE MUMMERS performing a Christmas play in the snow outside one of the village houses. The ornate ironwork is distinctive.

SHERBORNE SCHOOL in 1922, a fairly large gathering in front of the school house. Note the particular credit claimed by the photographer on this occasion (Butt of Bourton).

HUNT MEET at New Barn Inn on the main A40, when the landlord was J. Mace (Foster of Burford, postmarked 1909).

SHERBORNE SCHOOLBOYS, winners of the cup in 1929–30. On the left is local schoolmaster Mr Demer (Butt of Bourton).

SHERBORNE ROVERS, the village team of 1947–8. Standing: Jack Herrin, Lionel Cambray, Ernie Larner (who is holding the ball in the earlier photo), Harry Taylor, Les Hayward, Walter Tufnell and David Margetts. In the middle row: Ron Hayward, local police constable Reynolds and Michael Howard. Seated: Bill Maunders, Bill Moore, Eric Saunders, Harry Shepherd and Donald Saunders (The Butt Studio).

A TEAM OF SIX OXEN ploughing near Windrush *c.* 1895. This photograph was reproduced in J.A. Gibbs' famous study of *A Cotswold Village* of 1898 (Taunt of Oxford).

WINDRUSH CHURCH, seen from the south. St Peter's has been described by one church authority as 'the most perfectly typical Cotswold church imaginable'. In this photograph the decorated Norman doorway can be seen and the proportions of the Perpendicular 'wool' tower appreciated to the full (Taunt & Co. 674).

THE MALT HOUSE, Edward Hayward tiling the roof, assisted by his son Arthur on the scaffolding. Sitting dressing the slates is younger son Tom whilst the village postman conveniently adds to the scene (A.H. Witchell, photographer, Windrush).

'WAR WORKERS' at Windrush. This striking view by a local photographer is typical of otherwise unrecorded village activity. On the left is Mrs Bunting and on the right Miss Cook, both from Windrush (Witchell of Windrush).

GREAT BARRINGTON. Two views of the main street through the village; the short terraces of cottages are a feature of this estate village (lower view Butt of Bourton).

BARRINGTON PARK, the other major country house in the Windrush family apart from Sherborne. The setting commands the river which was landscaped as part of the parkland created for the house when it was built in 1736–8. This view shows the porch and Victorian wings added to the house in the early 1870s (Foster of Burford).

BARNS AT MANOR FARM, Great Barrington *c.* 1893, with farm labourers filling in time for the photographer (Taunt of Oxford).

TEACHERS AT GREAT BARRINGTON SCHOOL at the turn of the century. Mr H. Barrett on the left was headmaster at the school for 43 years until 1925 and was also organist and choirmaster in the village for 57 years until his death in 1940. Two of the other three teachers are Miss Wheeler and Miss Woods, both standing (C.J. Saunter of Stow).

GREAT BARRINGTON SCHOOL in 1898 – the Infants Department, with Miss Wheeler in charge (William Hooper, 22 Merton Street, New Swindon).

BARRINGTON CLUB with a full complement lined up for this photograph on Whit Monday, 25 May 1931. Seated on the ground is Mr Barrett who, besides his other village activities, was Club Secretary for over 50 years from its inception in 1887 until his death. At its jubilee celebrations in 1937, a dinner and a cricket match were held plus a dance, and the club's achievements recorded for posterity (Butt of Bourton).

SMALLEST HOUSE IN THE VILLAGE of Great Barrington, now demolished. It stood opposite the school and one of the village pumps was situated in the foreground to the left of the cottage. 'The one-up, one-down' accommodation was locally known as 'the beginners' because it was frequently let to newly married couples! (Frank Packer of Chipping Norton).

COACH TOUR in 1923 from the Barringtons and area to either Weston-super-Mare or Clevedon. This just pre-dates the formation of the local Women's Institute in 1925 (Alf Hardwick, The Studio, Banwell, Somerset).

FORMATION MEETING of the Barrington WI, held at Barrington Grove in 1925. Standing are Mrs Soule, Mrs Jenny Tidmarsh with baby Fred, Mrs Hayward who kept the village shop in Little Barrington, Miss Ruby Read, –?–, Mrs Griffin of Barrington Mill (at the rear), the Misses Hilda and Edith Pitts, Miss Lizzie Hall, Miss Dolly Adams with Miss Dorothy Cooper behind and Mrs Cantwell with her young child. Seated are the Misses Elinor and Margaret Godley of Barrington Grove, the County WI VCO from Gloucester and Mrs Ruby Lazenby.

LITTLE BARRINGTON village looking up towards the village green from the lane to Great Barrington. For the figures on the right, the caption reads 'Mrs Wakefield with pram and myself, Florrie Jones' (Frank Packer of Chipping Norton).

LITTLE BARRINGTON, another village view (Frank Packer of Chipping Norton).

LITTLE BARRINGTON CHURCH, another of the well-known church studies by Taunt. St Peters stands slightly away from the village on the road to Burford and is set on a bank, involving steps down into the porch and again into the nave (Taunt & Co. 796).

HOME FARM, Little Barrington, *c.* 1914 and home of Col. A.R. Hurst, lord of the manor of Little Barrington from 1905 until his death in 1948 (Foster of Burford).

SUN DIAL COTTAGE at Little Barrington *c*. 1900 (Foster of Burford).

ALICE HAYWARD in 1910 (then aged 3½ yrs) with brothers Arthur and Tom at the back door to the village shop in Little Barrington kept by their mother.

SUNDAY SCHOOL group with sewing ladies at Barrington Grove in the 1920s.

CORONATION line-up of Little Barrington villagers outside the parish hall on 2 June 1953 (Butt Studio).

GREAT RISSINGTON, a scene in the centre of the village close to the triangular green, and an example of a postcard view which circulated for years after the original photograph was taken (Butt of Bourton).

THE MANOR at Great Rissington, with the church on the right and part of a group of the main village buildings at the foot of the street. Largely seventeenth century with twentieth century enlargements, it stands on a 600-year-old site (Percy Simms of Chipping Norton).

CORONATION CELEBRATION CRICKET MATCH at Great Rissington on 12 May 1937. At the back: Harry Bartlett, Harry Pratley, Harry Mills, Jack Pratley, Dick Clifford, Gilbert Smith and an unknown umpire. In the front: Ted Packer, Bill Pill, George Rachael, Dick Timms, Fred Shergold and Harry Agg (Butt of Bourton).

MANOR COTTAGES, formerly the Old Manor House at Little Rissington until a new manor house was built in 1856. It was recorded as the largest house in the village in 1672 (Butt of Bourton).

LITTLE RISSINGTON, the centre of the village as the main street steadily climbs the hill from Bourton-on-the-Water. A horse-drawn delivery van makes its rounds. On the left, the thatched ricks are prominent (Butt of Bourton and G. East, Photographer, Post Office, Lower Slaughter).

WYCK RISSINGTON, the village as seen from the church tower (postmarked 1909).

COTTAGE, otherwise unidentified in the village of Wyck Rissington – a charming study set off by the ladies posing for the photographer (postmarked 1908).

CLAPTON SCHOOL c. 1905 outside the building provided in 1896. From this small group, at least two boys (the Wheeler brothers standing second left in the back row and sitting first left in the front row) were killed in the Great War, at the ages of 21 and 20 respectively. (C.T. Saunter of Stow).

CLAPTON CHURCH, One of the smallest of the Cotswold churches, but beautifully situated and full of simplicity. The stone-clad turret is a particular feature (Butt of Bourton).

COTTAGES forming a row at the top of the village. They were replaced in the 1950s by a similar row of council houses, including a post office (postmarked 1908).

STRAWBERRY PICKERS at Clapton in 1934. Commercial growing of strawberries began in the village between the wars, allowing local people to earn casual income in the summer months at Mr & Mrs Handy's farm. Ladies from Sherborne and Windrush can be identified in this group (Butt of Bourton).

SECTION FIVE

Upper and Lower Slaughter

UPPER SLAUGHTER, the village centre with the tower of St Peter's church amongst the farm houses and cottages of this archetypal Cotswold scene (East of Lower Slaughter).

UPPER SLAUGHTER, the well-known village scene with the tiny river Eye, a tributary of the Windrush providing the combination of water with local stone buildings which is such an attractive combination. The cottage alongside the crossing of the stream was demolished in the 1950s. The small village chapel is also typical of its type in the lower and earlier view dated c. 1898 (East of Lower Slaughter and Taunt of Oxford).

ROSE ROW of cottages at Upper Slaughter with the date recorded as 22 March 1914 (Butt of Bourton).

CHURCH OF ST PETER at Upper Slaughter seen from beside the Eye Brook, in a view subsequently obscured by the growth of trees (East of Lower Slaughter, postmarked 1932).

VILLAGE FÊTE on Wednesday 8 September 1920 at Copse Hill, just outside Upper Slaughter and the residence of Lt. Col. E.P. Brassey, DSO, MC. On this occasion the community was also celebrating the opening of a new parish hall and reading room by Mrs Broome Witts to commemorate the ending of the Great War. A presentation of medals to ex-servicemen was made by Baroness de Tuyll. Remarkably, all 54 men of the village who went to the War returned safely (Butt of Bourton).

MAY DAY childrens' festivities and maypole dancing on 1 May 1933 (Butt of Bourton).

'UPPER SLAUGHTER SAYS LONG LIVE KING GEORGE VI'. The assembled crowd outside this fine Manor House must have included virtually everybody in the village. The house is full of detail, set on sloping ground and originally with three gables to each façade in its sixteenth century form. Early in the seventeenth century, the two-storey porch was added and a fourth gable just visible on the right of this picture was added in 1913 when the house was enlarged.

MANOR HOUSE, seen here from the gardens on its west and south fronts after the enlargements of 1913 (East of Lower Slaughter).

CELEBRATIONS in 1950 for the Upper Slaughter WI with Miss Taylor, Miss Witts (cutting the birthday cake), Miss Desborough, Mrs Butler and Mrs Grey marking the occasion.

IN THE BROOK, alongside the corn mill at Lower Slaughter in 1933 with Tom Wilkins the miller relaxing his horse in the Eye Brook (East of Lower Slaughter).

TWO CLASSIC LOWER SLAUGHTER SCENES recorded on photographs and postcards for several generations. The village mill, a nineteenth-century building partly in stone and partly in brick, commands the scene and – like nearby Bourton – the attractive stone bridges across the brook provide an aesthetic pleasure. These are two views in a series of village scenes published as postcards by G. East at the Post Office in Lower Slaughter.

LOWER SLAUGHTER POST OFFICE, a view perhaps even better known than the two previous scenes in this series by East, who did not have far to travel to take this photograph. The weathered stone bridge provides a focal point. Within living memory the pure water supply to the village came from a nearby spring and was piped to a drinking fountain, dated 1875, just around the corner.

VILLAGERS gather on a footbridge across the brook for the occasion of a photograph (Collett of Bourton).

VILLAGE HALL, on the left and opened in 1887; beyond the old School House of a decade or so earlier, converted into a house *c.* 1932–4 (East of Lower Slaughter).

LOWER SLAUGHTER, another well composed study showing the church spire to full advantage (Powell of Bourton-on-the-Water).

FÊTE IN THE GROUNDS OF LOWER SLAUGHTER MANOR on 17 July 1920, the family home of the Whitmores for over three centuries until the estate was sold up in 1964 (Butt of Bourton).

THRESHING AT LOWER SLAUGHTER. The horse-drawn portable engine is being moved into position for threshing operations amongst the ricks.

SLAUGHTERS UNITED. Expressions with a purpose for the cup competition of 1920–1 (Butt of Bourton).

CUP TIE SEASON, with plenty of friendly rivalry at Slaughter on 2 April 1921 (Butt of Bourton).

AT THE CUP FINAL in Slaughter a week later on 9 April. The farm wagon, of typical Cotswold type, is being used in the traditional way as a grandstand by the supporters. Some favours are evident, but so too is the cold weather judging by overcoats and caps (Butt of Bourton).

ANOTHER FARM TROLLEY serves the same purpose to provide a good viewpoint for the crowd of all ages (Butt of Bourton).

MORE FOOTBALL FEVER. This time the presentation of the Hospital Cup to Bourton Rovers FC at Lower Slaughter on 17 April 1920 by local squire W.A. Rixon of Turkdean (Butt of Bourton).

LOWER SWELL c. 1900. The photographer must have been delighted with this composition, a combination of village scene and leisure activity with the Golden Ball Inn on the left. Barn and hayrick are as much village features as the cottages on the roadside.

SPA COTTAGES alongside the road from Stow to Lower Swell. A spring belonging to these cottages was discovered in 1807 to be rich in mineral deposits and a spa house with elaborate oriental decoration was added to one of the cottages. Hopes of prosperity for nearby Stow failed to materialise and the project developed no further (Clift & Ryland of Stow).

SECTION SIX

Stow-on-the-Wold

FOSSE WAY approaching Stow, with the Unicorn Hotel and posting house prominent at the junction with Sheep Street, *c.* 1890. This was one of the town's main inns in the nineteenth century, its gazebo window commanding views not only along the Fosse Way but also down the road towards Lower Swell and Cheltenham.

POST OFFICE at the corner of Church Street and Sheep Street, the other end of the group of buildings from the Unicorn Hotel (Clift & Ryland of Stow, postmarked 1909).

STOW SQUARE, the focal point of community life since the town was founded as a commercial enterprise by the abbey of Evesham in the eleventh century. Stow stands at a major road junction and its potential as a market was obvious, the wide market place confirming a determined attempt to develop this potential. By the late fifteenth-century there were two annual fairs. In 1477 King Edward IV authorised fairs on 24 October and 12 May; the feast days of St Philip and St James and of St Edward the Confessor. This view looks across the Square towards St Edward's church, with the town stocks an interesting surviving feature under the tree (W. Dennis Moss of Cirencester).

ST EDWARD'S HALL, built in the Square in 1878 as a public meeting place. Funds for its construction came from the proceeds of a Provident Bank established for the benefit of the town earlier in the century. Demolition of two houses was required and the removal of the town weighbridge. The bell turret to house the town's fire bell was added a few years later as a memorial to E.T. Godman for his public service to Stow (Taunt & Co 654).

STOW COURTHOUSE, in the corner of the Square at the junction with Church Street. This sixteenth-century building was demolished in 1899 and the corner site rebuilt the following year. Delapidation is obvious in this photograph which was probably taken for the record immediately prior to demolition. The town's lock-up was entered from the pavement through the small doorway on the right.

THE MARKET PLACE OR SQUARE on the southern side; two contrasting views of the same scene at least 40 years apart. The major difference is the removal in 1930 of the Cross House in the upper photograph, part of the groups of buildings which had encroached upon the open market place in medieval times. Gorton's and later French's Stores occupy the site of the courthouse. On the left is the Talbot, largest hotel in Stow by this date. The fifteenth century Market Cross was restored in 1878 and a plaque records the details; its protective railings were 're-cycled' during the Second World War (upper: Clift & Ryland, postmarked 1906; lower: Butt of Bourton).

THE CROSS. An earlier view c. 1885 and soon after its restoration. J.H. Alden's business produced some of Stow's earlier and most interesting postcards (Taunt of Oxford).

ST EDWARD'S HOUSE, with its unusual façade of Corinthian pilasters of the early eighteenth century – a charming oddity (Frank Packer of Chipping Norton).

THE SQUARE seen from the church tower and capturing something of the character of this attractive focal point to Stow life. Fosseway House can be seen on the far left (Alden of Stow).

ANOTHER CORNER OF THE SQUARE with largely nineteenth-century façades, *c.* 1938 (Clift & Ryland of Stow).

ALBERT HYDE'S CYCLE AND REPAIR SHOP in the Square with a range of period bicycles on display. The business was founded around 1900 following Mr Hyde's employment as a tinsmith in the foundry of Hollis & Son, agricultural implement makers elsewhere in the Square. Note the Cyclists Touring Club sign and the Crown & Anchor Inn next door.

FEBERY'S BUTCHERS SHOP a few doors away from Hyde but some years later in 1922, with (from the left) Mr Blandford Febery; Mr Jefferies, a horse breaker; Miss Allchurch, the housekeeper and Mr H. Venner, the assistant butcher.

STOW CHURCH INTERIOR (Butt of Bourton).

HUNT MEET in the Square at Stow, a popular gathering place for the Heythrop Hunt. The upper view is earlier (postmarked 1913) with the Manor House the surgery and residence of the town's doctor. In the lower view St Edward's Hall can be appreciated occupying a dominant position in the market place (upper: J.W. Farrell of Stow).

PARK STREET at the junction of Digbeth Street with Sheep Street. On the left is one of the oldest buildings in Stow, dating from the sixteenth century and with a porch added in 1615 (Clift & Ryland of Stow).

ODDINGTON ROAD and the main route east from Stow to Oxford. The town's turnpike gate was situated here and the toll-house survives. The Bell Inn fills the junction with the minor road to Maugersbury.

STOW POST OFFICE. The staff in 1913, with, standing from the left: J.H. Webb, S. Lockey, J.H. Woodward, L.W. Appleton, Miss K.M. Ryland, J.C. Acock, C. Faulkner, C. Hoare, Miss P.R. Gibbs, E. Perkins and H.B. Bridges. In the front: Miss F.A. Fisher, Miss A.A. Fisher the postmistress and Miss M.B. Stroud.

WATER SUPPLY in Stow was a problem throughout the nineteenth century, until lord of the manor Joseph Chamberlayne-Chamberlayne donated £2,000 in 1871 for the provision of a water supply and a deep well was bored. Until then the water cart was a familiar sight between Well Lane and the town, and no doubt carried on being used in later years. Well Lane was also a popular walking destination for Stow folk at their leisure.

STOW STATION, a companion timber-framed building to that erected at Bourton-on-the-Water at or soon after the line was opened from Kingham in 1862. Both were replaced by Cotswold stone station buildings in the 1930s.

STOW CLUB. The Oddfellows and Conservative Benefit Society meets in the Square on 7 June 1920. As with other Cotswold friendly societies, Club Day consisted of a church parade, a dinner at the Unicorn and a procession to the sports field (Butt of Bourton).

STATION ROAD at Stow in the years before the First World War when traffic was not a problem. The station coach waits outside the Unicorn Hotel in case of trade (James H. Alden, Printer and Publisher, Stow-on-the-Wold).

STOW FAIR *c.* 1905, one of several street fairs and markets held in Cotswold towns since the Middle Ages, and one of the best known. By the eighteenth century over 20,000 sheep were sold at each of the two annual fairs. Subsequently Stow Fair became better known as a horse fair and here a large number of horses are lined up along the Fosse Way looking towards Stow Hill from the junction of Sheep Street. Agricultural implements are also for sale (C.T. Saunter of Stow).

ANOTHER VIEW OF STOW HORSE FAIR in Station Road with horses lined up for inspection, not least by members of the local Jefferies family of farmers and dealers.

ACCOMPANYING THE BUSINESS WAS A PLEASURE FAIR held in the market place and a reminder of the traditional gathering for such activities. The funfair aspect is still preserved in the 'mop' fairs of the autumn months (C.T. Saunter of Stow).

SILVER JUBILEE. Planting a tree alongside the town's drinking fountain to celebrate the 25 years' reign of George V on 6 May 1935. The fountain (presented in 1896) has since been moved across the road. The tree continues to flourish (Butt of Bourton).

QUAR WOOD, a Gothic mansion in the grand style, built for Revd R.W. Hippisley in 1857 but rebuilt virtually as a new house between 1954 and 1958 (Clift & Ryland of Stow).

NETHER SWELL MANOR, close to Stow, although outside the parish, and another house in the grand style. A carefully-executed example of Cotswold style and created c. 1909–13, when it was the home of W.M. Scott, a leading breeder of pedigree shorthorns and Berkshire pigs. The architect was Sir Guy Dawber (Butt of Bourton).

A STOW FAMILY, proudly posing outside their home with a sailor son (J.W. Farrell of Stow).

WEDDING GROUP FROM STOW or one of the local villages (J.W. Farrell of Stow).

GEORGE HATHAWAY in retirement at Stow, holding the heart-shaped collecting tin of the old Bledington Morris Dance side. The tin survives and so too do the traditions preserved by George Hathaway's generation of Morris Men in Bledington, Longborough and other Cotswold villages.

CHURCH FÊTE for Stow, held at Maugersbury Manor in 1927 (Frank Packer of Chipping Norton).

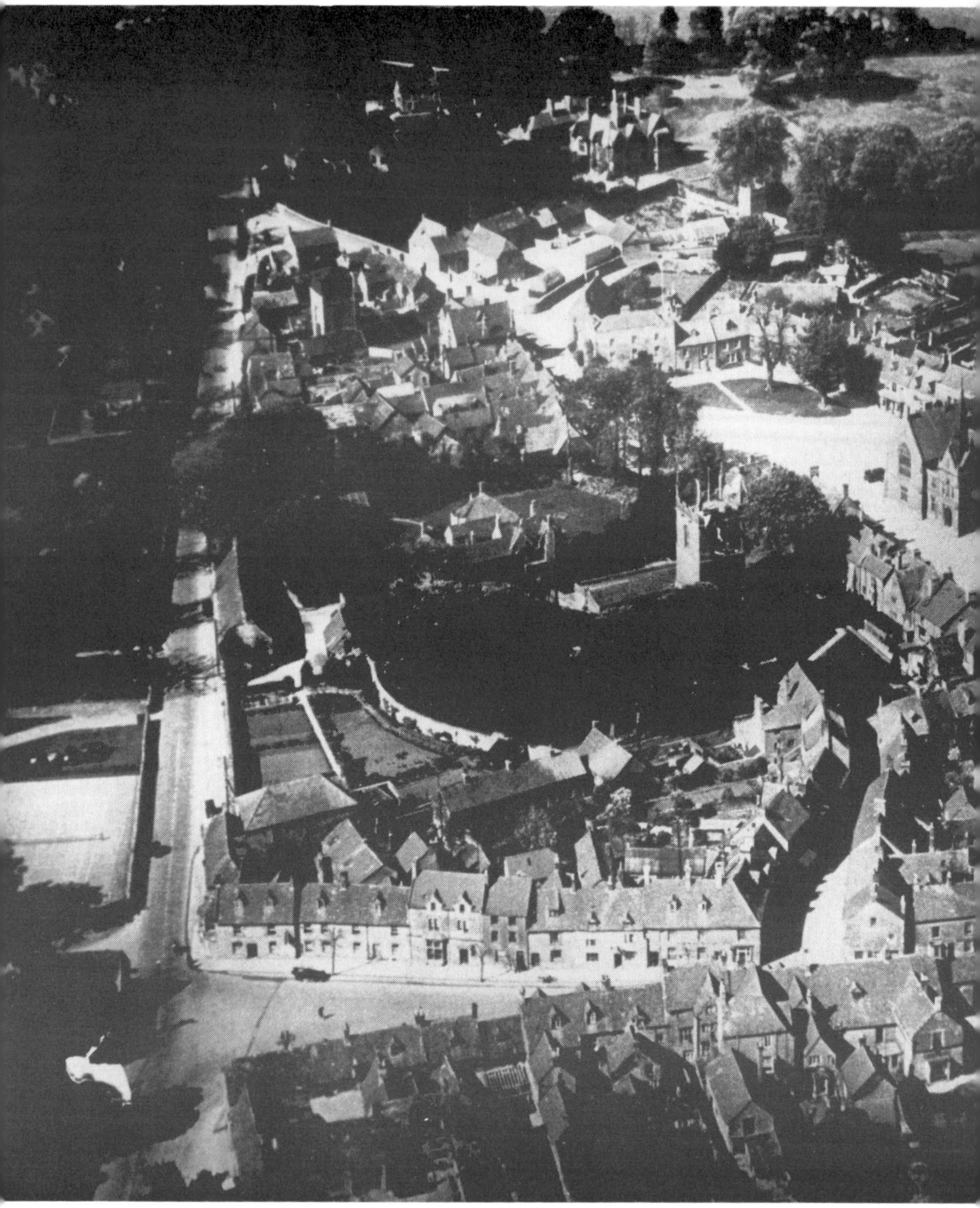

AERIAL VIEW OF STOW c. 1930 with the Fosse Way clearly defined on the left and Sheep Street in the foreground. The Square is equally prominent with the surviving group of buildings in its centre; a reminder of earlier infilling now removed. The church is centrally placed, and much of the town plan continues to reflect a pattern established at least by the seventeenth century.

ACKNOWLEDGEMENTS

An album of this kind cannot be completed without the support of a great many people, particularly as the compiler set out deliberately to locate as much previously unpublished material as possible and to reflect something at least of the character of each of the venues included here. If he succeeded it is in no small part due to the kindness and co-operation with which this venture was received, and thanks are due to all those who without exception allowed their family collections to be raided for this purpose. In setting me on the right course with much useful material and contacts for Northleach, Bourton-on-the-Water and Stow-on-the-Wold, I am especially grateful to Bill Fallows, David Stratford and Bob Sharp respectively, and this is an opportunity to give them acknowledgement for their sterling researches over the years in the fine traditions of the local historian. For Northleach, I owe thanks for the loan of photographs to Mrs Carol Coates, Bob Cook, and 'Chequer' Barrett and to John Norman of Charlton Kings and Mrs Webb of Cirencester. For Gerald Green's enthusiasm for Northleach and knowledge of the town's development I am especially grateful, as well for his own photographs.

It is also a pleasure to record the wealth of local detail and photographs made available by the following: Mr & Mrs P. Pratley of Bourton-on-the-Water; Mr Jim Lazenby of Little Barrington; Mrs Alice Williams of the same village but now of Northleach; Mr Jim Humphries of Bourton-on-the-Water but now of Little Rissington; Mr Alan Wheeler and family of Lower Slaughter, including Mrs Taylor; and for Sherborne, Walter and Mrs Tufnell, Mrs Longhurst and Mrs George. For great generosity with their postcard collections, I thank Phil Griffiths of Cirencester and Freda Gittos of Edwardian Postcards. My research was greatly helped by access to the local studies collection of the Bingham Library at Cirencester and by the considerable Cotswold knowledge of David Day of Moreton in Marsh, who also generously contributed the Introduction. John Gibbons of Uffington copied a great deal of material in a short time with his usual cheerfulness and efficiency.

Where the photographic collections of the Corinium Museum of Cirencester and the Cotswold Countryside Collection at Northleach cover the area of this volume they have been used, and considerable appreciation is due to those many donors over the years whose photographs are preserved in this public archive. A complete list is not possible, but especial thanks are due to those whose pictures are used here including Norman Irvine of Cirencester, David Hicks, Mrs Westmacott, Mrs Hayward of Birmingham, Mrs Yates, Mr & Mrs Hewer of Northleach, Mrs D. Day of Chedworth, Mr D.W. Burge of Shipston on Stour and the Cheltenham Art Gallery & Museum. Mr H. Pickett of Maidstone very generously rehabilitated a splendid group of Cotswold postcards. Derek White and Trevor Radway have been generous in their provision of material, and access has always been freely given to the collections held by the Museum of English Rural Life at the University of Reading, the Gloucestershire Records Office, the Oxford City Library, the Wilts & Glos Standard and the Packer Studio in Chipping Norton (the latter now housed at the Oxfordshire County Museum at Woodstock).

A full list of the source of photographs used in this album is maintained at the Cotswold Countryside Collection at Northleach where the compiler would be grateful to receive additional information or photographs as well as corrections to the information given in the captions. His best thanks are due to the staff of the Cotswold Museum Service for their support and encouragement.

Finally and without question most important, David Viner wishes to acknowledge his considerable debt of gratitude to the Sly family of Northleach, Enid, Joyce and Llewelyn, for their unfailing courtesy in making available a rich source of Northleach material to form the major part of the Northleach section in this volume. If the town gains more than a fair share of space in these pages, it is due largely to their enthusiasm and to the compiler's determination that its history should be brought to a wider attention and enjoyment than has perhaps been possible in the past.

David Viner

Cotswold Countryside Collection
Northleach
1 September 1987